EXPLORING • SPACE

Probing Space

David Baker and Heather Kissock

WEIGL PUBLISHERS INC.

Published by Weigl Publishers Inc.
350 5th Avenue, Suite 3304, PMB 6G
New York, NY 10118-0069

Website: www.weigl.com

All of the Internet URLs given in the book were valid at the time of publication. However, due
to the dynamic nature of the Internet, some addresses may have changed, or sites may have
ceased to exist since publication. While the author and publisher regret any inconvenience this
may cause readers, no responsibility for any such changes can be accepted by either the
author or the publisher.

Library of Congress Cataloging-in-Publication Data

Baker, David, 1944-
Probing Space / David Baker and Heather Kissock.
    p. cm. -- (Exploring space)
 Includes bibliographical references and index.
 ISBN 978-1-60596-025-8 (hard cover : alk. paper) --
 ISBN 978-1-60596-026-5 (soft cover : alk. paper)
1. Space probes--Juvenile literature. I. Kissock, Heather. II. Title.
TL795.3.B35 2010
629.43'4--dc22

                              2009001920

Printed in China
1 2 3 4 5 6 7 8 9 0 13 12 11 10 09

Weigl would like to acknowledge Getty Images and NASA as its primary photo suppliers
for this title.

Every reasonable effort has been made to trace ownership and to obtain permission
to reprint copyright material. The publishers would be pleased to have any errors
or omissions brought to their attention so that they may be corrected in
subsequent printings.

EDITOR: Heather Kissock
DESIGN: Terry Paulhus

Probing Space

CONTENTS

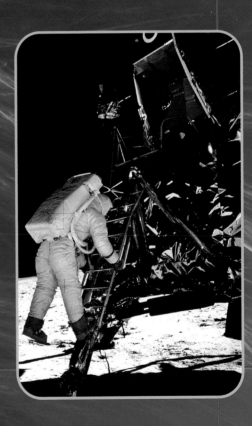

What is a Space Probe?

A space probe is an unmanned vehicle that is sent to explore planets and other bodies beyond Earth's **atmosphere**. It is equipped with specialized computers and **robotics** that can guide it to specific locations in space, obtain information about its mission, and send that information back to Earth. Space probes have contributed greatly to human space exploration.

Space probes explore planets and other space bodies that are millions of miles from Earth. Technology has not advanced to a point where people can visit these planets. Instead, scientists have sent probes into space to gather information and relay it back to Earth. Space probes have sent back much information about the planets, moons, and other space bodies in our solar system. Due to probes, scientists have learned about the materials and gases that make up many of these space bodies. Probes have also been used to prepare the Moon for human occupation.

Probes are monitored at mission control centers all over the world. Scientists track their progress and receive the information the probes send back.

Several probes have landed on Mars. Mars Pathfinder landed there in 1997, and took hundreds of pictures of the planet's surface.

One of the most recent probes to land on Mars is the Phoenix Mars Lander. It arrived on the surface of Mars on May 25, 2008 to collect information about the planet.

BRAIN BOOSTER

Space probes can travel at speeds up to 13 miles (21 kilometers) per second.

A space probe can operate in one of three ways. Some space probes fly by planets and other space bodies, collecting a range of information as they go. Others **orbit** a planet, obtaining detailed information on that planet over the long term. A space probe can also land on a planet and collect data to send back to Earth.

Prob
a Prob

Probes have many components to help them reach their scientific goals. First of all, they are equipped with technology that allows them to gather the information scientists need and to send that information to Earth. They also have components that allow them to maneuver through space and reach their destinations safely.

COMMUNICATIONS SYSTEMS
Radios, receivers, and transmitters all work to receive and send information to scientists on Earth.

POSITIONING SYSTEMS
This equipment guides the probe and keeps it on course. It also helps position instruments so that the correct readings can be taken.

DATA HANDLING
Computers and **detectors** collect information and take any readings the mission requires.

POWER
Solar panels and batteries keep the electronics systems on board the probe running. They also keep the probe moving through space.

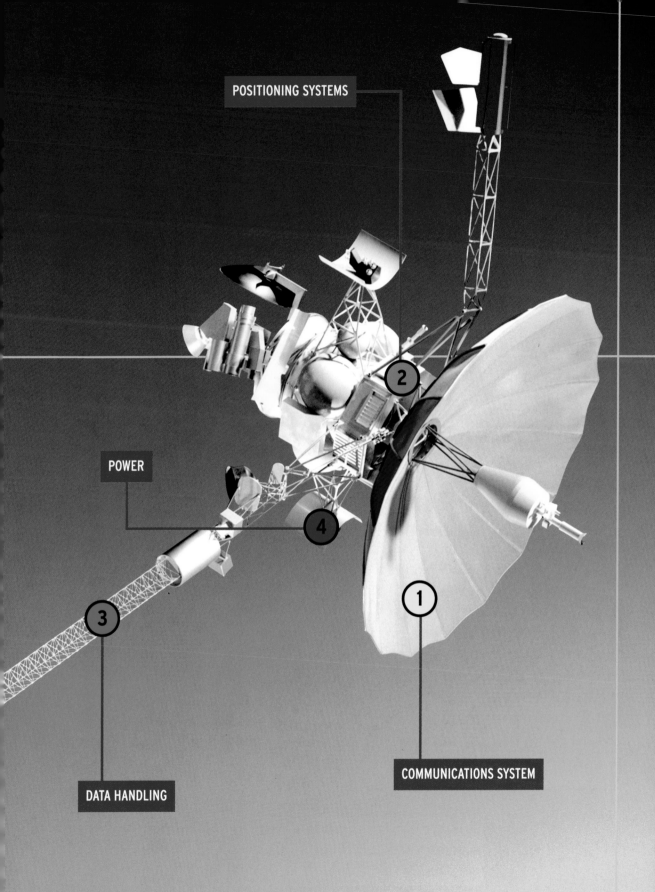

POSITIONING SYSTEMS

POWER

DATA HANDLING

COMMUNICATIONS SYSTEM

The Big Push

Space probes, and other large spacecraft, need a big push to travel into space. The biggest part of the push occurs at the beginning of the journey, when the spacecraft is launched. Earth's **gravity** keeps pulling on the probe, trying to keep it on the ground. The spacecraft must have enough force of its own to escape gravity. The only spacecraft known to have this capability is the rocket. Space probes rely on rockets to take them out of Earth's atmosphere.

Rockets are long, tube-shaped objects that carry fuel and oxygen. Oxygen is used to burn the fuel. When the fuel begins to burn, gases are released out the bottom end of the rocket. The force of these gases creates the **thrust** needed to push the rocket in the opposite direction. This propels the rocket, and its cargo, into space. Rockets are used to send everything from probes to space shuttles into space.

To escape from Earth's gravity, rockets must reach a speed of at least 25,000 miles (40,234 km) per hour.

NASA built the shuttle, a reusable space plane, in the 1970s. It was designed to carry equipment, such as probes, into space and return to Earth, where it could be used again. Several probes have been taken into space inside shuttles.

In many cases, probes are attached directly onto a rocket for launching. However, when a space shuttle takes a probe into space, it is stored in the shuttle's cargo bay. Once the shuttle is far away from Earth, the cargo bay doors are opened, and the probe is launched. The probe then relies on its own power source to travel through space.

The shuttle was used to send a probe called *Galileo* to Jupiter in 1989.

THINK ABOUT IT Rockets are the only known way to send objects into space. Can you think of another way to do this? Draw a diagram showing the device you would develop to send objects into space.

Traveling
the Galaxy

Countries first started sending probes into space in the 1950s. They were developed as part of the space race between the United States and Russia. The two countries were competing to see who could put a person on the Moon. Space probes were sent to the Moon to find out more about it. At first, the probes only flew by the Moon, but by 1959, a probe had landed on the Moon's surface.

In the 1960s, attempts were made to send probes to Earth's neighbor planets, Mars and Venus. The first probe, Mariner 1, failed shortly after launch, but Mariner 2 successfully launched and flew by Venus. In 1964, Mariner 4 flew by Mars.

Mariner 2 was launched on August 27, 1962. It arrived at Venus on December 14 of the same year.

With this success, scientists began developing probes that could travel farther away from Earth. The first space probe sent to any of the **outer planets** was launched in 1972. Called Pioneer 10, it flew by Jupiter one year later. Since then, probes have passed by Saturn, Neptune, and Uranus, taking pictures and sending them back to Earth.

Probes have continued to be a first point of contact for most space missions. They are sent to planets and other space bodies before humans or any other equipment. As technology has developed, the probes have become more specialized and are now able to provide scientists with a wider range of information. This helps scientists learn more about the universe and the role Earth plays in it.

In 1973, Pioneer 10 flew by Jupiter and took pictures of the planet's Great Red Spot. This huge storm is about 17,000 miles (28,000 km) long and 9,000 miles (14,000 km) wide. It was discovered in 1664.

GET CONNECTED

For a complete list of space probe missions, view the timeline at www.spacetoday.org/History/ ExplorationTimeLine.html.

Lunar
Probing

On September 13, 1959, Russia's Luna 2 space probe became the first humanmade object to land on the Moon. It crashed onto the Moon's surface. This proved to scientists that the Moon had no **radiation belts** and almost no **magnetic field**. If it had, the probe would have been destroyed before it could reach the Moon's surface. This information helped scientists plan future Moon missions.

Many more probes have been sent to the Moon since Luna 2. As countries fine-tuned their technology, the probes were able to survive a Moon landing and send information back to Earth. Much of this information has come in the form of pictures. These images have allowed scientists to map the Moon and learn more about its surface and environment.

The ability of **lunar** probes to land safely on the Moon proved that the Moon's surface could hold heavy equipment. This information was used to plan human landings on the Moon. The first humans landed on the Moon on July 20, 1969, 10 years after the first probe landing.

Buzz Aldrin was one of the first humans to step foot on the Moon.

Visiting an Old Friend

Crews continued to land on the Moon for many years after the first landing. However, over time, the focus of space exploration shifted to developing new technologies, such as space shuttles and space stations. Visits to the Moon decreased as a result.

This situation changed in 2004 when U.S. President George W. Bush announced a return to Moon exploration. He planned to build a research base there. The first part of this plan is to send probes to the Moon to prepare for later crewed missions. The probes will research the living environment, as well as potential locations for the base.

A lunar probe is set to launch in 2009. Called the Lunar Reconnaissance Orbiter, it has been designed to find safe landing and living sites. It will also look for areas with low radiation levels and usable natural resources, mainly water. All of these are needed for humans to land, live, and survive on the Moon.

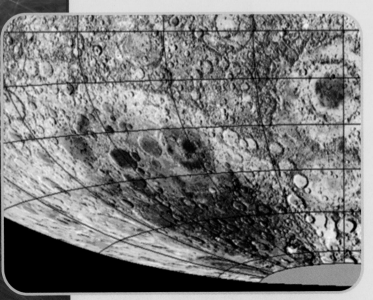

One of the Lunar Reconnaissance Orbiter's jobs is to locate water on the Moon. Scientists believe the South Pole is a likely location for water.

Setting a Path
for the Sun

There are many reasons for scientists to study the Sun. The Sun is the center of the **solar system** and the largest star within it. It provides Earth with light, warmth, and a power source. As part of **photosynthesis**, sunlight provides life support for almost every living thing on Earth. As well, energy radiating from the Sun creates many of the weather systems occuring on Earth. Studying the Sun can help scientists gain a better understanding of Earth itself.

Much of the research performed by probes has focused on the Sun's magnetic field and its solar winds. In fact, the first probes sent to study the Sun in the 1960s took measurements and studied the activities of these two features. This data allowed scientists to develop theories about how things that happen on the Sun, such as **solar flares** and **coronal holes**, affect weather and climate on Earth and elsewhere in the solar system.

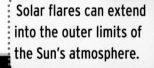
Solar flares can extend into the outer limits of the Sun's atmosphere.

Solar Probe+ will travel closer to the Sun than any previous spacecraft.

In the next few years, scientists plan to develop probes that can travel closer to the Sun. NASA is putting together a probe called Solar Probe+. Its mission will be to fly into the Sun's corona, or atmosphere. The goal of the mission is to find out how the Sun generates its heat and how solar winds gather speed. This information will help scientists predict space weather and plan crewed space missions around poor traveling conditions.

BRAIN BOOSTER

Solar Probe+ is scheduled to go on its first mission in 2015.

The Sun's magnetic field is believed to reach the dwarf planet Pluto. Pluto is 3,674 million miles (5,913 million kilometers) from the Sun.

Hello
Neighbors

The four planets closest to the Sun—Mars, Earth, Venus, and Mercury—are known as the inner planets. As more probes were sent to study the Sun, scientists turned their attention to the inner planets. Mars, Venus, and Mercury became the new destinations for probes.

In the early 1960s, the United States and Russia began sending probes to Mars and Venus. These are the two planets closest to Earth. Scientists wanted to know what features they shared with Earth and if either planet could support human life.

The Venera probes were the first probes to send pictures from the surface of Venus.

Venus was the first planet to have a probe examine it. This occurred in 1962, when Mariner 2 performed a flyby. The probe took several types of readings. Some readings were related to the planet's environment. Venus was found to have a very hot surface. However, the heat lost its strength higher up in the atmosphere. A few years later, Russia was able to land a series of probes on Venus. These Venera probes studied the rocks and other materials that made up the planet's surface.

Mars, however, was the first planet to be photographed by a probe. Launched in 1964, Mariner 4 was the first probe to successfully fly by Mars. Up to this time, scientists had believed that Mars' environment was like that of Earth. Images sent from the probe proved these theories wrong. Mars was shown to be a harsh, barren land that could not support human life in the same way that Earth can. Over time, probes were landing on the planet and taking readings on its atmosphere, climate, and soil. As a result of this research, scientists began planning to send astronauts to Mars to study it further.

There are no plans to put humans on Mercury. It is too close to the Sun to be able to support human life. The only probe to fly by the planet was Mariner 10 in 1974. It mapped parts of the planet and studied its atmosphere, showing that Mercury has extreme temperature shifts. Temperatures can be as high as 800° Fahrenheit (427° Celsius) during the day, but they can sink to -295°F (180°C) at night.

In 2004, NASA sent a probe called MESSENGER to Mercury to study the planet. It is expected to begin orbiting the planet in 2011.

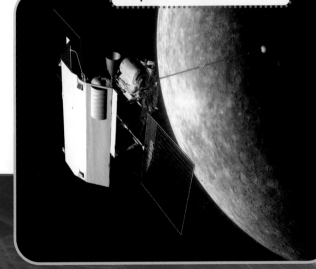

GET CONNECTED

To learn more about the MESSENGER space probe and its mission, go to messenger.jhuapl.edu.

Distant Relatives

The success of the inner planet probes led scientists to send probes to the outer planets as well. The first outer planet to have a probe fly by was Jupiter, in 1973. Pioneer 10 took pictures and readings of Jupiter and its moons. It was followed by two more probes, Voyager 1 and Voyager 2, in 1979. Voyager 1 sent images showing that one of Jupiter's moons, Io, had volcanic activity on its surface. This was something Pioneer 10 had not noticed.

After flying by Jupiter, Voyager 1 journeyed to Saturn. Arriving there in 1980, it studied materials within the planet's rings and the structure of them. Once Voyager 1 completed its flyby of Saturn, it continued into the far reaches of the solar system, where it still travels today.

Voyager 2 followed its flyby of Saturn with visits to Neptune and Uranus. It passed by Uranus first, where it located 10 new moons and sent back data on the planet's atmosphere and rings. Three years later, in 1989, Voyager 2 reached Neptune's orbit. There, it performed research on the planet's rings and calculated the planet's **mass**.

Voyager 1's images have shown scientists that Saturn has at least 100 separate rings.

New Horizons

After it studies Pluto, New Horizons will continue its journey into deep space and send information about what it finds back to scientists on Earth.

For many years, the solar system had nine planets. However, in 2006, scientists decided that Pluto was not large enough to be a planet. It was reclassified a **dwarf planet** instead. It still, however, held the interest of scientists, and a plan to send a probe was put in motion.

The probe, New Horizons, will be the first spacecraft ever to travel to Pluto. Launched in 2006, it is expected to reach Pluto in 2015. New Horizons will map Pluto's surface and look for clues about how the planet formed.

Visting Guests

Besides major space bodies, such as the Sun, the planets, and their moons, probes have also been sent on missions to study other space bodies. **Comets** and **asteroids** can be found throughout the solar system, traveling through space on orbits of their own. Some comets and asteroids are familiar to scientists. This is because their orbits are short and they pass by Earth on a regular basis. Other asteroids and comets are less well known. Their orbits are longer, and it can take them millions of years to complete their path.

One of the best-known comets is Halley's comet. As a short orbit comet, it passes by Earth about every 75 years. Halley's comet is one of the few comets that can be seen without the aid of telescopes. People have been viewing it since 240 BC. Its long history with humans is one of the reasons why scientists have sent technology into space to study it.

Russia was one of the first countries to have probes observe Halley's comet. Vega 1 and 2 joined the comet's orbit in 1986. They took more than 500 images of the comet. These images and other readings helped scientists gauge the comet's size.

Halley's comet is expected to pass by Earth again in 2061.

Tempel 1 was traveling at about 23,000 mph (37,100 kmph) when Impactor collided with it.

The European Space Agency's probe, Giotto, also followed the comet. Giotto was able to get closer to the comet than the other probes. As a result, it was able to study the comet in more detail. Tests determined that the comet is at least 2.5 billion years old. It is made up mainly of dust and ice, and is shaped like a peanut.

Scientists are interested in the materials that make up comets and asteroids. They can learn much about the creation of the solar system by studying them. In 2005, scientists purposely had a probe called Impactor collide with the Tempel 1 comet so that they could find out more about the comet's components. The mission showed scientists that the comet was made up of ice and **organic** materials.

THINK ABOUT IT What other types of space bodies can probes study? If you could send a probe anywhere in the universe, where would you direct it to go? Why?

Making
the Grade

Working with space probes requires people to have very specific skills and education. Probe specialists must have a good grasp of science principles, along with strong technical skills. They must be detail-oriented people who strive to improve current technologies, With these traits and qualifications, there are many career paths that can be taken.

ASTRONAUTICAL ENGINEER

Astronautical engineers design, develop, and test spacecraft, including probes. They often specialize in very specific areas, such as structural design and navigation or communication systems. It is their job to create equipment and vehicles that can survive the journey from Earth to space and back again. They need to have expert knowledge on the conditions the equipment will experience so that the correct materials and technology are used to create it. They are involved in the construction process from design to finished product.

ASTRONAUT QUALIFICATIONS

CITIZENSHIP

Pilots and **mission specialists** must be U.S. citizens. **Payload specialists** can be from other countries.

EDUCATION

Astronauts must have a minimum bachelor's degree in engineering, biology, physics, or mathematics. Most astronauts have a **doctorate**.

SOFTWARE ENGINEER

Space probe software engineers make computer programs that operate inside the probes. These programs may help with the probe's navigation system or with the work that the probe is in space to do, such as measure magnetic fields and solar winds. Once these programs are developed, the software engineer will make sure that they work properly, testing them from time to time, and correcting or improving any parts of the program that are not working well.

LAUNCH MANAGER

A launch manager is the person who prepares to launch a probe into space. Launch managers schedule the launch process. The launch manager arranges for a launch vehicle, such as a rocket or space shuttle, to carry the probe into space. He or she must make sure that the vehicle is large enough and strong enough to carry the probe into space. Launch managers arrange to transport the probe to the launch site. They must have a good understanding of the probe development process, as well as NASA's safety standards, so that the launch process runs smoothly and safely.

EXPERIENCE	HEALTH	HEIGHT
Astronauts must have at least three years of experience in a science-related field. Pilots must have jet experience with more than 1,000 hours of in-command flight time.	All astronauts must pass a NASA physical, with specific vision and blood pressure requirements.	Pilots must be 64 to 76 inches (162.5 to 193 cm) tall. Mission or payload specialists must be 58.5 to 76 inches (148.5 to 193 cm) tall.

A Day
in Space

When a space shuttle takes a probe into space, releasing the probe is just one job in a day that has a firmly set schedule. Flight controllers on Earth wake up the crew in the morning with a pop song that they blast over the shuttle's speakers. For breakfast, astronauts eat a meal that they chose before launch. Each meal is labelled with the astronaut's name and the day it should be eaten. After eating, it is time for the astronauts to get ready for work.

A list, known as the flight plan, tells the crew what they are to work on each day. Sometimes, there is the need for a spacewalk. Other times, the crew carries out housework duties, such as trash collection and cleaning. Breaks, such as lunch and dinner, are scheduled throughout the day. Keeping fit in such a small space is very important. Blocks of time are put aside for the astronauts to exercise. At the end of the work day, the astronauts may read a book or listen to music.

The Daily Schedule

8:30 to 10:00 a.m.: Post-sleep (Morning station inspection, breakfast, morning hygiene)

10:00 to 10:30 a.m.: Planning and coordination (Daily planning conference and status report)

10:30 a.m. to 1:00 p.m.: Exercise (Set-up exercise equipment, exercise, and put equipment away)

1:00 to 2:00 p.m.: Lunch, personal hygiene

2:00 to 3:30 p.m.: Daily systems operations (Work preparation, report writing, emails, to-do list review, trash collection)

3:30 to 10:00 p.m.: Work (Work set-up and maintenance, performing experiments and payload operations, checking positioning and operating systems)

10:00 p.m. to 12:00 a.m.: Pre-sleep (food preparation, evening meal, and hygiene)

12:00 to 8:30 a.m.: Sleep

The work that astronauts do on the shuttle is serious, but there is always time to enjoy the experience of being in space.

Teamwork is an essential part of space shuttle life.
Astronauts live in a confined space for days. They must all work together to make the trip comfortable for everyone on board.

Beyond the
Solar System

While some probes return to Earth following their missions, others continue traveling deeper into space. Often, they continue sending images and other information back to Earth. In time, scientists hope these probes will show them what lies beyond our solar system.

After they completed their mission to the outer planets, Voyager probes 1 and 2 continued their journey through space. They are both heading for an area called the heliopause. This is the point where the solar system ends and **interstellar** space begins. Based on solar wind data from Voyager 1, scientists believe the probe began closing in on this area in 2004. It will enter interstellar space first, with Voyager 2 following a few years later. Voyager 2 is traveling in the opposite direction so that it can give scientists a different view of the journey. It may take up to 20 years for the probes to pass through the heliopause.

The Voyager probes were launched within one month of each other. Voyager 2 was launched on August 20, 1977. Voyager 1 lifted off on September 5 of the same year.

Sirius is part of a constellation called *Canis Major*, or Greater Dog. For this reason, it is sometimes called the "dog star."

Both probes are believed to have enough power to continue operating until 2020. At that time, Voyager 1 will be 12.4 billion miles (19.9 billion km) away from the Sun, and Voyager 2 will be 10.5 billion miles (16.9 billion km) away. While neither probe is on a specific course, Voyager 2 is on track to pass by Sirius, the brightest star in the night sky. This, however, would not happen for at least 296,000 years.

BRAIN BOOSTER

Voyager 1 is currently traveling through the heliosphere. This is the area that leads into the heliopause. It is still within the Sun's magnetic field.

Scientists have used high-powered telescopes to study other **galaxies**. These telescopes have helped them predict the amount of time it will take Voyager 2 to reach Sirius.

Test Your Knowledge

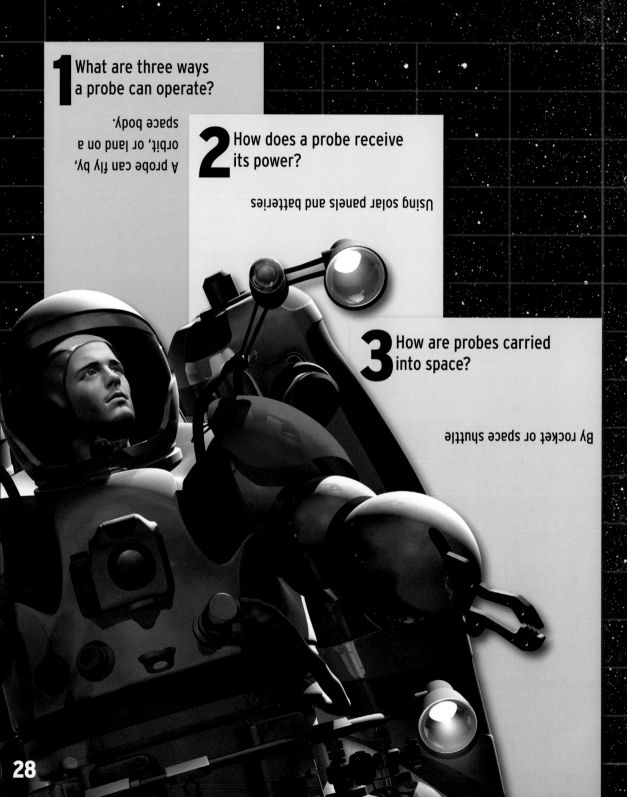

1 What are three ways a probe can operate?

A probe can fly by, orbit, or land on a space body.

2 How does a probe receive its power?

Using solar panels and batteries

3 How are probes carried into space?

By rocket or space shuttle

4 When did countries start sending probes into space?

The 1950s

5 What was the first humanmade object to land on the Moon?

A Russian probe called Luna 2

6 How far does the Sun's magnetic field reach?

At least to Pluto, which is 3,674 million miles (5,913 million km) from the Sun

7 Name the four inner planets.

Mercury, Venus, Mars, Earth

8 Which probe is scheduled to reach Pluto first?

New Horizons

10 What is the heliopause?

The area where the solar system ends and interstellar space begins

9 How long have people been viewing Halley's comet?

Since 240 BC

Further
Resources

Many books provide information about space exploration. To learn more about other technology used to explore space, try reading these books.

Baker, David, and Heather Kissock. *International Space Station*. New York, NY: Weigl Publishers Inc., 2010.

Baker, David, and Heather Kissock. *Rockets*. New York, NY: Weigl Publishers Inc., 2009.

Bocknek, Jonathan. *Telescopes*. New York, NY: Weigl Publishers Inc., 2003.

Websites

To get the latest info on the Voyager probes, go to **http://voyager.jpl.nasa.gov/index.html**.

Current developments on the New Horizons probes can be accessed at **http://pluto.jhuapl.edu**.

To read about other probes that have been sent into space, visit **www.worldspaceflight.com/probes**.

Glossary

asteroids: rocks that orbit the Sun

atmosphere: the layer of gases that surrounds Earth

comets: objects made up of rock, water, and ice that orbit the Sun

coronal holes: parts of the Sun's atmosphere that have lower temperatures and densities

detectors: mechanical sensing devices

doctorate: an advanced university degree

dwarf planet: a space body that orbits the Sun and is large enough to assume a nearly round shape, but does not clear the neighborhood around its orbit

galaxies: star systems held together by gravity

gravity: a force that moves things toward the center of a planet

interstellar: between or among stars

lunar: relating to the Moon

magnetic field: a field of force around a magnet or moving, charged particle

mass: the amount of matter in a body

mission specialists: scientists sent into space by NASA

NASA: National Aeronautics and Space Administration; the United States' civilian agency for research into space and aviation

orbit: to move in a path around a planet or other space object

organic: chemicals containing carbon

outer planets: the space bodies farthest away from the Sun; Jupiter, Uranus, Neptune, and Saturn

payload specialists: scientists sent into space by companies or countries other than the United States

photosynthesis: the process a plant uses to combine sunlight, water, and carbon dioxide to produce oxygen and sugar

radiation belts: ring-shaped regions around a planet in which electrically charged particles are trapped

robotics: the research area concerned with robots

solar flares: bursts of solar gases from the Sun's surface

solar panels: structures built to attract the Sun's rays so that power can be produced

solar system: the Sun together with the eight planets and all other bodies that orbit the Sun

thrust: the force that occurs when an object is pushed

Index